UNMANNED GROUND VEHICLE USING A GSM NETWORK

ADWITYA PRADHAN || SACHIN GURURANI || ASHISH KUMAR

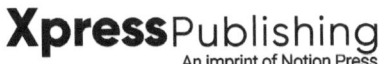

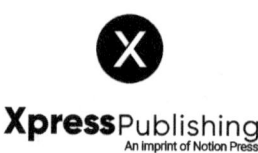

XpressPublishing
An imprint of Notion Press

Old No. 38, New No. 6
McNichols Road, Chetpet
Chennai - 600 031

Copyright © Adwitya Pradhan || Sachin Gururani || Ashish Kumar
All Rights Reserved.

ISBN 978-1-64892-761-4

This book has been published with all efforts taken to make the material error-free after the consent of the author. However, the author and the publisher do not assume and hereby disclaim any liability to any party for any loss, damage, or disruption caused by errors or omissions, whether such errors or omissions result from negligence, accident, or any other cause.

While every effort has been made to avoid any mistake or omission, this publication is being sold on the condition and understanding that neither the author nor the publishers or printers would be liable in any manner to any person by reason of any mistake or omission in this publication or for any action taken or omitted to be taken or advice rendered or accepted on the basis of this work. For any defect in printing or binding the publishers will be liable only to replace the defective copy by another copy of this work then available.

Contents

1. Unmanned Vehicle — 1
2. Introduction — 2
3. Unmanned Ground Vehicle – Using Gsm Network With Microcontroller — 7
4. System Overview — 9
5. Hardware Design Framework — 11
6. Gsm — 20
7. Component Details — 27
8. Circuit Design — 28
9. Construction And Working — 29
10. Software Design Framework — 31
11. Control Flow Diagram — 33
12. Program Code — 34
13. Experimental Results — 36
14. Cost Analysis — 37
15. Application — 39
16. Example — 43
17. Emergency Response — 46
18. Future Scope — 47
19. Conclusion — 48
20. Bibliography — 49

CHAPTER ONE

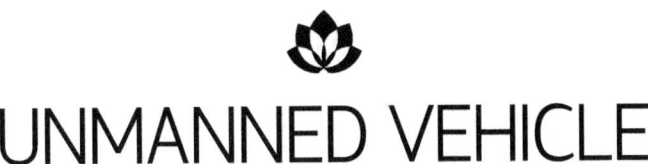

UNMANNED VEHICLE

An uncrewed vehicle or unmanned vehicle is a vehicle without a person on board. Uncrewed vehicles can either be remote controlled or remote guided vehicles, or they can be autonomous vehicles which are capable of sensing their environment and navigating on their own.

These are the following types of unmanned vehicles or uncrewed vehicle:-

- Unmanned Ground Vehicles (UGV), such as autonomous car or DTMF car.
- Unmanned Aerial Vehicles (UAV), such as drone.
- Unmanned Surface Vehicles (USV), for the operation of the surface water.
- Unmanned Underwater Vehicles (UUV), such as underwater drone.

CHAPTER TWO

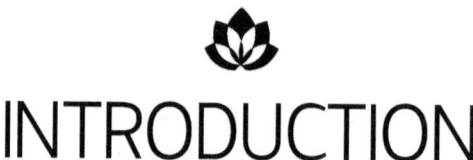

INTRODUCTION

An unmanned ground vehicle (UGV) is a vehicle that operates while in contact with the ground and without an on-board human presence. UGVs can be used for many applications where it may be inconvenient, dangerous, or impossible to have a human operator present. Generally, the vehicle will have a set of sensors to observe the environment, and will either autonomously make decisions about its behaviour or pass the information to a human operator at a different location who will control the vehicle through teleoperation.

The UGV is the land-based counterpart to unmanned aerial vehicles and remotely operated underwater vehicles. Unmanned robotics are being actively developed for both civilian and military use to perform a variety of dull, dirty, and dangerous activities.

Unmanned Ground Vehicle - History

A working remote controlled car was reported in the October 1921 issue of RCA's World Wide Wireless magazine. The car was unmanned and controlled wirelessly via radio, it was thought the technology could someday be adapted to tanks. In the 1930s, the USSR developed Tele tanks, a machine gun-armed tank remotely controlled by radio from another tank. These were used in the Winter War (1939-1940) against Finland and at the start of the Eastern Front after Germany invaded the USSR in 1941. During World War II, the British developed a radio control version of their Matilda II infantry tank in 1941. Known as "BlackPrince", it would have been used for drawing the fire of concealed anti-tank guns, or for demolition missions. Due to the costs of converting the transmission system of the tank to Wilson type gearboxes, an order for 60 tanks was cancelled.

From 1942, the Germans used the Goliath tracked mine for remote demolition work. The Goliath was a small tracked vehicle carrying 60 kg of explosive charge directed through a control cable. Their inspiration was a miniature French tracked vehicle found after France was defeated in 1940. The combination of cost, low speed, reliance on a cable for control, and poor protection against weapons meant it was not considered a success.

The first major mobile robot development effort named Shakey was created during the 1960s as a research study for the Defence Advanced Research Projects Agency for Artificial Intelligence (DARPA-AI) to test its obedience with commands, which is different from advanced robots that are autonomous or semi-autonomous. Shakey was a wheeled platform that had a TV camera, sensors, and a computer to help guide its navigational tasks of picking up wooden blocks and placing them in certain areas based on commands.

Unmanned Ground Vehicle - Today

Russia and China are expeditiously becoming a commander in Unmanned Ground Vehicle development. Russia has a wide range of planarity armed war robots. China is looking not only at circumventing American dominance in military robotics, but also consolidating the regional advantage. A series of hot territorial disputes between China and its neighbours stimulates military investments in Tokyo, Seoul and Singapore.

Unmanned Ground Vehicle - Design

Based on its application, unmanned ground vehicles will generally include the following components: platform, sensors, control systems, guidance interface, communication links, and systems integration features.

1. **Platform:-** The platform can be based on an all-terrain vehicle design and includes the locomotive apparatus, sensors, and power source. Tracks, wheels, and legs are the common forms of locomotion. In addition, the platform may include an articulated body and some are made to join with other units.
2. **Sensors:-** A primary purpose of UGV sensors is navigation, another is environment detection. Sensors can include compasses, odometers,

inclinometers, gyroscopes, cameras for triangulation, laser and ultrasound range finders, and infrared technology.
3. **Control Systems:-** Unmanned ground vehicles are generally considered Remote-Operated and Autonomous, although Supervisory Control is also used to refer to situations where there is a combination of decision making from internal UGV systems and the remote human operator.
4. **Remote Operated:-** Unmanned ground vehicles are generally considered Remote-Operated and Autonomous, although Supervisory Control is also used to refer to situations where there is a combination of decision making from internal UGV systems and the remote human operator.

Some example of the remote operator UVG are:

- Unmanned Snatch Land Rover.
- Frontline Robotics Tele operated UGV (TUGV).
- Gladiator Tactical Unmanned Ground Vehicle (used by the United States Marine Corps).
- iRobot PackBot.
- Unmanned ground vehicle Milo's used by Serbian Armed Forces.
- Foster-Miller TALON.
- Remotec ANDROS F6A.
- Autonomous Solutions.
- Mesa Associates Tactical Integrated Light-Force Deployment Assembly (MATILDA).
- Vecna Robotics Battlefield Extraction-Assist Robot (BEAR).
- G-NIUS Autonomous Unmanned Ground Vehicles (Israel Aerospace Industries/Elbit Systems joint venture) Guardium.
- Robowatch ASENDRO.
- Ripsaw MS1.
- DRDO Daksh.
- VIPeR.
- DOK-ING mine clearing, firefighting, and underground mining UGV's.
- MacroUSA Armadillo V2 Micro UGV (MUGV) and Scorpion SUGV.
- Nova 5.
- Krymsk APC.

5. Autonomous:- An autonomous UGV is essentially an autonomous robot that operates without the need for a human controller. The vehicle uses its sensors to develop some limited understanding of the environment, which is then used by control algorithms to determine the next action to take in the context of a human provided mission goal. This fully eliminates the need for any human to watch over the menial tasks that the UGV is completing.

A fully autonomous robot may have the ability to:

- Collect information about the environment, such as building maps of building interiors.
- Detect objects of interest such as people and vehicles.
- Travel between waypoints without human navigation assistance.
- Work for extended durations without human intervention.
- Avoid situations that are harmful to people, property or itself, unless those are part of its design specifications.
- Disarm, or remove explosives.
- Repair itself without outside assistance.

A robot may also be able to learn autonomously. Autonomous learning includes the ability to :

- Learn or gain new capabilities without outside assistance.
- Adjust strategies based on the surroundings.
- Adapt to surroundings without outside assistance.
- Develop a sense of ethics regarding mission goals.

Autonomous robots still require regular maintenance, as with all machines.

One of the most crucial aspects to consider when developing armed autonomous machines is the distinction between combatants and civilians. If done incorrectly, robot deployment can be detrimental. This is particularly true in the modern era, when combatants often intentionally disguise themselves as civilians to avoid detection. Even if a robot maintained 99% accuracy, the number of civilian lives lost can still be catastrophic. Due to this, it is unlikely that any fully autonomous machines will be sent into battle armed, at least until a satisfactory solution can be developed.

Some examples of autonomous UGV technology are:

- Vehicles developed for the DARPA Grand Challenge.
- Autonomous car.
- Multifunctional Utility/Logistics and Equipment vehicle.
- Crusher developed by CMU for DARPA.

- **Guidance Interference:-** Depending on the type of control system, the interface between machine and human operator can include joystick, computer programs, or voice command.
- **Communication Links:-** Communication between UGV and control station can be done via radio control or fibre optics. It may also include communication with other machines and robots involved in the operation.

- **System Integration:-** Systems architecture integrates the interplay between hardware and software and determines UGV success and autonomy.

CHAPTER THREE

UNMANNED GROUND VEHICLE – USING GSM NETWORK WITH MICROCONTROLLER

Radio frequency control is the use of radio signals to remotely control a device. The term is used frequently to refer to the control of model vehicles from a handheld radio transmitter. Industrial, military, and scientific research organizations make use of radio-controlled vehicles as well. A remote control vehicle (RCV) is defined as any mobile device that is controlled by a means that does not restrict its motion with an origin external to the device. This is often a radio control device, cable between control and vehicle, or an infrared controller. A RCV is always controlled by a human and takes no positive action autonomously.

The IR system follows the line of site approach of actually pointing the remote at the device being controlled; this makes communication to be impossible over obstacles and barriers. Moreover since IR systems suffer from these problems so to overcome this; a signalling scheme utilizing voice frequency tones is employed. This scheme is known as Dual Tone Multi-Frequency (DTMF), Touch-Tone or simply tone dialling. As its acronym suggests, a valid DTMF signal is the sum of two tones, one from a low group (697-941Hz) and the other from a high group (1209-1633Hz) with each group containing four individual tones. DTMF signalling plays an important role in distributed communication systems such as multiuser mobile radio. It is natural in the two way radio environment since it slips nearly into the centre of the voice spectrum, has excellent noise immunity and it has a highly integrated method of implementation currently available. It is directly compactable with telephone signals simplifying automatic phone batch system.

The development of silicon implemented switch capacitors, sample-1 filters, marks the current generation of DTMF receiver technology. Initially single chip band pass filters were combined with currently available decoders enabling a two chip receiver design. A further advance in integration has merged both functions onto a single chip allowing DTMF receivers to be realized in minimal space of a low cost. Most Nokia phones have F-Bus and M-Bus connections that can be used to connect a phone to Personal Computers (PC) or in this case, a microcontroller. The connection can be used for controlling just about all functions of the phone.

In this paper, phones using GSM network interfaced with a microcontroller is used to remotely control an unmanned robotic vehicle thus overcoming distance barrier problem and communication over obstacles with very minimal or no interference but is solely network dependent. We present the design and implementation of an unmanned vehicle (i.e. a robotic vehicle) consisting of a GSM network (a mobile phone), DTMF decoder, microcontroller and a motor driver. The transmitter is a handheld mobile phone. Ordinary low cost mobile phones like Nokia 1100 or even older versions of Nokia phones could be used effectively for this purpose. There is no special requirement on the part of the mobile phones both of which are used in the transmitter and receiver section respectively.

CHAPTER FOUR

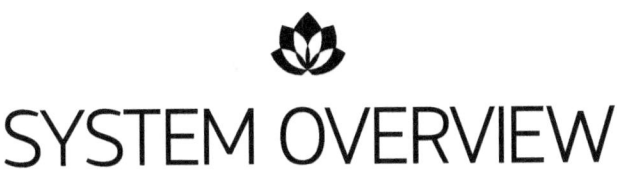

SYSTEM OVERVIEW

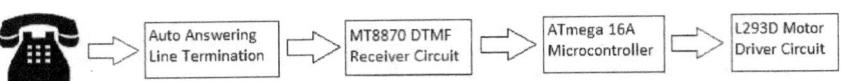

Figure1 DTMF Data Communication Architecture

The diagrams in fig.1 and fig.2 describe the overall system. Here the robotic vehicle is controlled by a mobile phone that makes a call to the GSM mobile phone attached to the robot. In the course of a call, if any button is pressed, a tone corresponding to the button pressed is heard at the other end of the call. This tone is called 'dual-tone multiple-frequency' (DTMF) tone. The robotic vehicle perceives this DTMF tone with the help of the phone stacked in the vehicle. The received tone is processed by the microcontroller with the help of DTMF decoder. The decoder decodes the DTMF tone into its equivalent binary digit and this binary number is sent to the microcontroller. The microcontroller is preprogramed to take a decision for any given input and outputs its decision to motor drivers in order to drive the motors for forward or backward motion or turn left or right. The mobile that makes a call to the mobile phone stacked in the vehicle acts as a remote. So this simple robotic vehicle does not require the construction of receiver and transmitter units, reducing the overall circuit complexity.

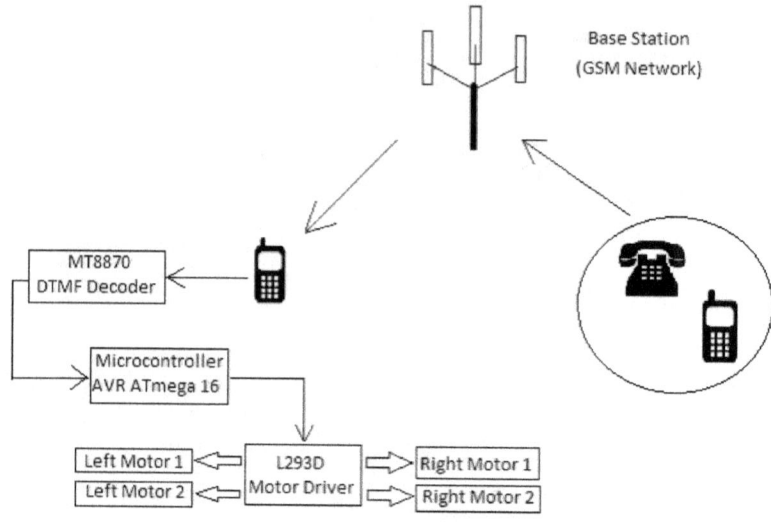

Figure 2 Functional block diagram of the system

CHAPTER FIVE

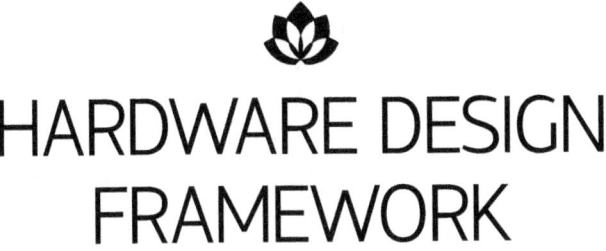

HARDWARE DESIGN FRAMEWORK

HARDWARE DESIGN FRAMEWORK

The blocks of the receiver model which is seen in fig.2 are explained in detail in this section:

DTMF DECODER

Dual-tone multi-frequency signalling (DTMF) is an in-band telecommunication signalling system using the voice-frequency band over telephone lines between telephone equipment and other communications devices and switching centres. DTMF was first developed in the Bell System in the United States, and became known under the trademark **Touch-Tone** for use in push-button telephones supplied to telephone customers, starting in 1963. DTMF is standardized as ITU-T Recommendation. It is also known in the UK as MF4.

The Touch-Tone system using a telephone keypad gradually replaced the use of rotary dial and has become the industry standard for landline and mobile service. Other multi-frequency systems are used for internal signalling within the telephone network.

Multifrequency Signalling

Prior to the development of DTMF, telephone numbers were dialled by users with a loop-disconnect (LD) signalling, more commonly known as pulse dialling (dial pulse, DP) in the U.S. It functions by interrupting the current in the local loop between the telephone exchange and the calling party's telephone at a precise rate with a switch in the telephone that is operated by the rotary dial as it spins back to its rest position after having been rotated to each desired number. The exchange equipment responds to the dial pulses either directly by operating relays, or by storing the number in a digit register recording the dialled number. The physical distance for which this type of dialling was possible was restricted by electrical distortions and was only possible on direct metallic links between end points of a line. Placing calls over longer distances required either operator assistance or provision of special subscriber trunk dialling equipment. Operators used an earlier type of multi-frequency signalling.

Multi-frequency signalling (MF) is a group of signalling methods that use a mixture of two pure tone (pure sine wave) sounds. Various MF signalling protocols were devised by the Bell System and CCITT. The earliest of these were for in-band signalling between switching centres, where long-distance telephone operators used a 16-digit keypad to input the next portion of the destination telephone number in order to contact the next downstream long-distance telephone operator. This semi-automated signalling and switching proved successful in both speed and cost effectiveness. Based on this prior success with using MF by specialists to establish long-distance telephone calls, dual-tone multi-frequency signalling was developed for end-user signalling without the assistance of operators.

The DTMF system uses a set of eight audio frequencies transmitted in pairs to represent 16 signals, represented by the ten digits, the letters A to D, and the symbols # and *. As the signals are audible tones in the voice frequency range, they can be transmitted through electrical repeaters and amplifiers, and over radio and microwave links, thus eliminating the need for intermediate operators on long-distance circuits.

AT&T described the product as "a method for pushbutton signalling from customer stations using the voice transmission path." In order to prevent consumer telephones from interfering with the MF-based routing and switching between telephone switching centres, DTMF frequencies differ from all of the pre-existing MF signalling protocols between switching centres: MF/R1, R2, CCS4, CCS5, and others that were later replaced by SS7 digital signalling. DTMF was known throughout the Bell System by the trademark Touch-Tone. The term was first used by AT&T in commerce on July 5, 1960 and was introduced to the public on November 18, 1963, when the first push-button telephone was made available to the public. It was a registered trademark by AT&T from September 4, 1962 to March 13, 1984. It is standardized by ITU-T Recommendation. In the UK, it is also known as MF4.

Other vendors of compatible telephone equipment called the Touch-Tone feature tone dialling or DTMF, or used their other trade names such as Digit one by Northern Electric Company in Canada.

As a method of in-band signalling, DTMF signals were also used by cable television broadcasters to indicate the start and stop times of local commercial insertion points during station breaks for the benefit of cable companies. Until out-of-band signalling equipment was developed in the 1990s, fast, unacknowledged DTMF tone sequences could be heard during the commercial breaks of cable channels in the United States and elsewhere. Previously, terrestrial television stations used DTMF tones to control remote transmitters.

Keypad

The DTMF telephone keypad is laid out as a matrix of push buttons in which each row represents the low frequency component and each column represents the high frequency component of the DTMF signal. There are four rows and usually three columns, though a fourth column may be present for some applications. Pressing a key sends a combination of the row and column frequencies. For example, the 1key produces a superimposition of a 697 Hz low tone and a 1209 Hz high tone. Initial pushbutton designs employed levers, enabling each button to activate one row and one column contact. The tones are decoded by the switching centre to determine the keys pressed by the user.

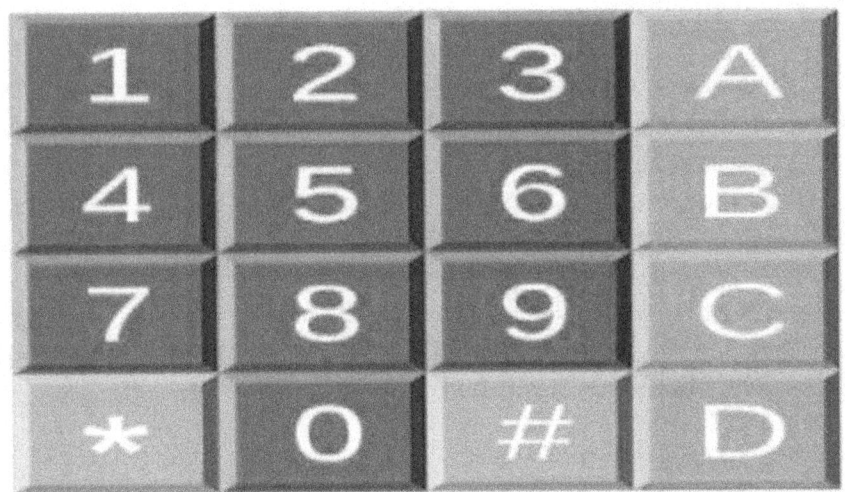

Keypad

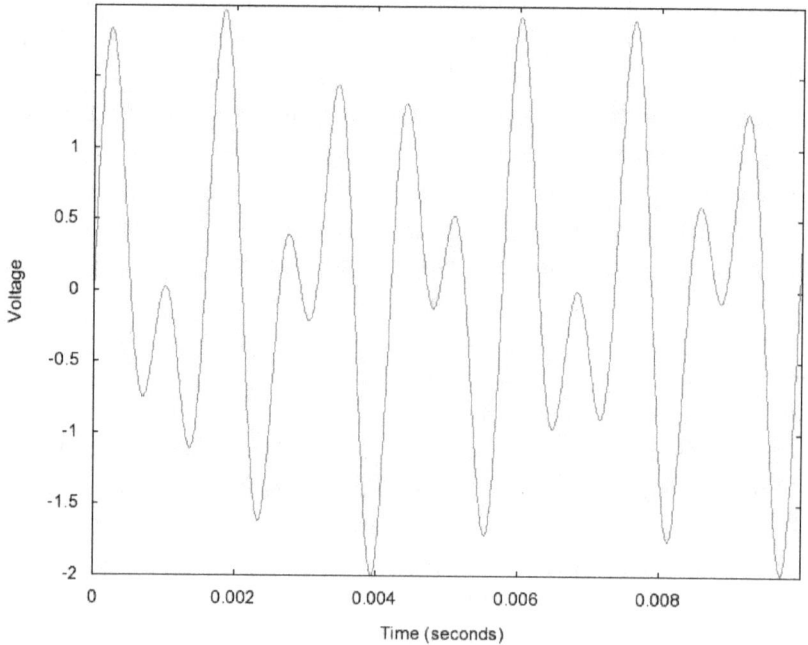

Combination of 1209 Hz and 697 Hz sine waves, representing DTMF 1

An MT8870 (Fig. 3) series DTMF decoder is used here. All types of the MT8870 series use digital counting techniques to detect and decode all the 16 DTMF tone pairs into a 4-bit code output. The built-in dial tone rejection circuit eliminates the need for pre-filtering. When the input signal given at pin 2 (IN-) in single-ended input configuration is recognized to be effective, the correct 4-bit decode signal of the DTMF tone is transferred to Q1 (pin 11) through Q4 (pin 14) outputs D0 through D3 outputs of the DTMF decoder (IC1) are connected to port pins of microcontroller.

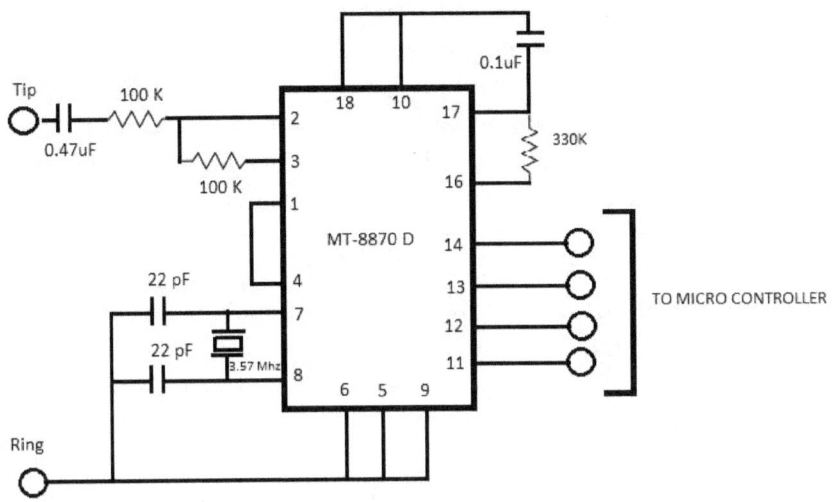

Figure 3

The MT8870 is a complete DTMF receiver, integrating both the band split filter and digital decoder functions. The filter section uses switch capacitor techniques for high and low group filters; the decoder uses digital counting techniques to detect and decode all 16 DTMF tone pairs into a 4 bit code. External component count is minimized by on chip provision of a differential input amplifier clock oscillator and latched three state bus interfaces. The functional description of the MT8870 is given in the following sections:

- **Filter Section**: Separation of the low group and high group tones is achieved by applying the DTMF signal to the input of the two sixth order switched capacitor band pass filter, the band width of which correspond to the low and high group frequencies. Each filter output is followed by a single order switched capacitor filter section which smoothens the signal prior to limiting; limiting is performed by high gain comparators which are provided with hysteresis to prevent detection of unwanted low level signals. The output of the comparators provides full rail logic swing at the frequency of the incoming DTMF signals.

- **Decoder Section**: Following the filter section is a decoder employing digital counting techniques to determine the frequencies of the incoming tones and to verify that they correspond to standard DTMF Frequencies. A complex averaging algorithm protects against tone simulation by extraneous signals such as voice while providing tolerance to small frequency deviations and variations. This averaging variation algorithm has been developed to ensure an optimum combination of immunity to talk off and tolerance to the presence of interfering frequencies (third tone) and noise. When the detector recognizes the presence of two valid tones (this is referred to as the signal condition, in some industry specifications) the early steering (E_{st}) output will go to an active state. Any subsequent loss of signal condition will course EST to assume an inactive state.

- **Steering Circuit**: Before registration of a decoded tone pair, the receiver checks for a valid signal duration (referred to as character recognition condition) this check is performed by an external Resistance Capacitance (RC) time constant E_{st}. Logic high on E_{st} causes collector voltage (V_c) to rise as the capacitor discharges. The time required to detect the presence of two valid tones top is function of the decode algorithm, the tone frequency and the previous state of the decode logic. EST indicates and initiates an RC timing circuit. If both tones are present for the minimum guide time (t_{CTP}) which is determine by the external RC network, the DTMF signal is decoded and the resulting data is latched in the output register. The delay steering (S_{tD}) output is raised and indicates that new data is available. The time required to receive a valid DTMF signal (T_{rec}) is equal to the sum of time to detect the presence of valid DTMF signals (t_{DP}) and guard time, tone present.

MOTOR DRIVER

The L293D is a quad, high-current, half-H driver designed to provide bidirectional drive currents of up to 600 mA at voltages from 4.5V to 36V. It makes it easier to drive the DC motors.

The L293D consists of four drivers. Pins IN1 through IN4 and OUT1 through OUT4 are input and output pins, respectively, of driver 1 through driver 4. Drivers 1 and 2, and drivers 3 and 4 are enabled by enable pin 1 (EN1) and pin 9 (EN2), respectively. When enable input EN1 (pin 1) is high, drivers 1 and 2 are enabled and the outputs corresponding to their inputs are active. Similarly, enable input EN2 (pin 9) enables drivers 3 and 4 [4], [5].

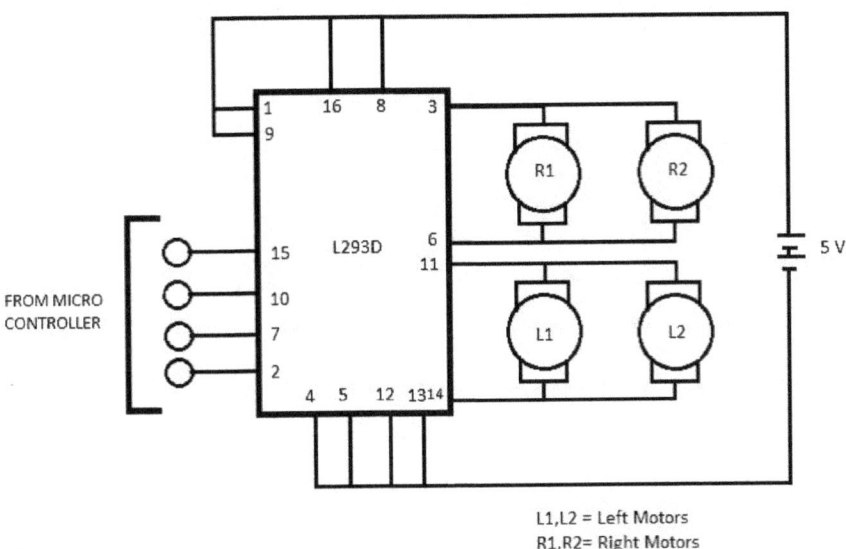

Figure 4

MICROCONTROLLER

The ATmega16 is a low-power CMOS 8-bit microcontroller based on the AVR enhanced RISC architecture. By executing powerful instructions in a single clock cycle, the ATmega16 achieves throughputs approaching 1 MIPS per MHz allowing the system designer to optimize power consumption versus processing speed.

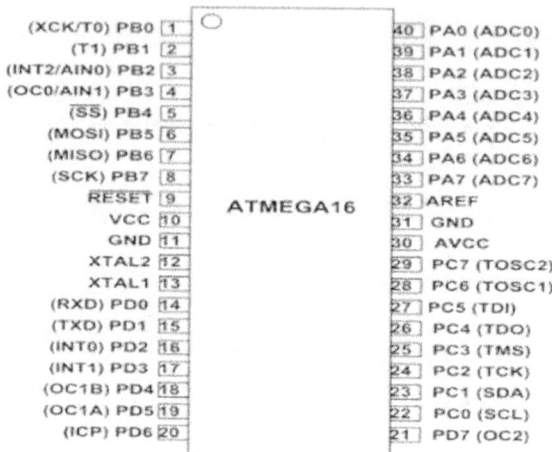

Figure 5

It provides the following features: 16 Kb of in-system programmable Flash program memory with read-while-write capabilities, 512 bytes of EEPROM, 1kB SRAM, 32 general-purpose input/output (I/O) lines and 32 general-purpose working registers. All the 32 registers are directly connected to the arithmetic logic unit, allowing two independent registers to be accessed in one single instruction executed in one clock cycle.

The resulting architecture is more code-efficient. The on-chip Flash allows the program memory to be reprogrammed in-system or by a conventional non-volatile memory programmer. By combining a versatile 8-bit CPU with Flash on a monolithic chip, the Atmel microcontroller is a powerful microcomputer, which provides a highly flexible and cost effective solution to many embedded control applications.

Outputs from port pins of the microcontroller are fed to inputs IN1 through IN4 respectively, to drive four geared DC motors. The microcontroller output is not sufficient to drive the DC motors, so current drivers are required for motor rotation.

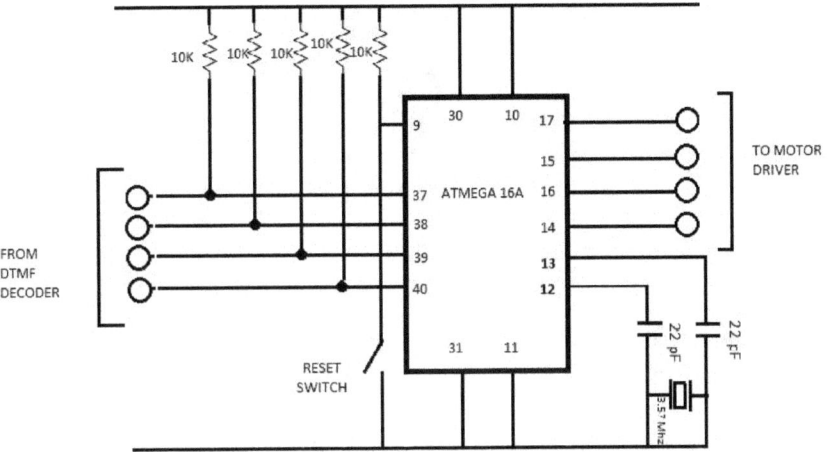

Figure 6

CHAPTER SIX

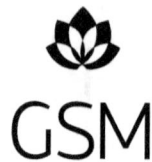

GSM

GSM (Global System for Mobile Communication)
   Technical Details
   Cellular Radio Network

GSM is a cellular network, which means that mobile phone connect to it by searching for cells in the in mediate vicinity. There are live different cell sizes in a GSM network – macro cell, microcell, Pico cell, Femto cell and umbrella cells.

- Macro cells can be regarded as cells where the base station antenna is installed on a mast or a building above average roof top level.
- Micro cells are whose antenna height is under average roof top level, they are typically used in urban areas.
- Pico cells are small cells whose coverage diameters are few dozen meters, they are mainly used indoors.
- Femto cells are cells is designed for use in residential or small business environment and connect to the service provider's network via a broadband internet connection.
- Umbrella cells are used to cover shadowed regions of smaller cells and fill in gaps in coverage between those cells.

Modulation Used In GSM

The modulation used in GSM in GMSK (Gaussian Minimum Shift Key), a kind of continuous phase frequency shift keying. In GMSK, the signal to be modulated onto the carrier is first smoothed with a Gaussian Low-Pass filter prior to being fed to a frequency modulator, which greatly reduces the interference to neighbouring channels (adjacent-channel interference).

Carrier Frequencies in GSM

GSM networks operate in a number of different carrier frequency ranges with most 2G GSM networks operating in the 900MHz or 1800MHz bands were used instead for example in Canada and the United States.

Regardless of the frequency selected by an operator, it is divided into timeslots for individual phones to use. This allows eight full-rate or sixteen half-rate speech channels per radio frequency. These eight radio timeslots are grouped into a TDMA frame. Half rate channels use alternate frames in the same timeslot. The channel data rate for all 8 channels in 270.833 Kbit/s, and the frame duration is 4.615 Mrs. The transmission powers in the handset powers in the handset is limited to a maximum of 2Watt in GSM 850/900 and 1Watt in GSM 1800/1900.

SIM (Subscriber Identity Module)

The SIM is detectable smart card containing the user's subscription information and phone book. This allows the user to retain his or her information after switching handsets. The user is an also change operations while retaining the handset simply by changing the SIM. Some operators will block this by allowing the phone to use only one SIM, this practice is known as SIM locking and is illegal in some countries.

GSM Network Structure

- MS (Mobile Station)
- BSS (Base Station Subsystem)
- NSS (Network Switching Subsystem)
- NMS (Network Management Subsystem)

GSM SYSTEM ARCHITECTURE

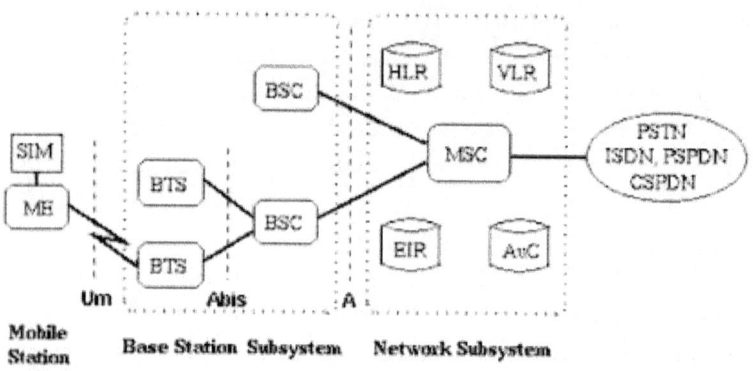

SIM Subscriber Identity Module   BSC Base Station Controller   MSC Mobile services Switching Center
ME   Mobile Equipment   HLR Home Location Register   EIR Equipment Identity Register
BTS Base Transceiver Station   VLR Visitor Location Register AuC Authentication Center

GSM SYSTEM ARCHITECTURE

MS (Mobile Station)

The MS (Mobile Station) is a combination of terminal equipment and subscriber data. The terminal equipment as such is called ME (Mobile Equipment) and the subscriber's data is stored in a separate module called SIM (Subscriber Identity Module). From the user's point of view, the SIM is certainly the best known database contains user specific identification. The SIM card can be taken out if one mobile equipment and inserted in to another. In the GSM network, the SIM card identifies the user just like a traveller uses a passport to identify himself. The SIM card contains the identification numbers of the user and a list of available networks. The SIM card also contains tools needed for authentication and ciphering. Depending on the type of the card, there is also storage space for messages, such as phone numbers.

BSS (Base Station Subsystem)

The Base Station Subsystem is a responsible for managing the radio network, and it is controlled by an MSC. Typically, one MSC contains several BSSs. A BSS itself may cover considerably large geographical are consisting of many cells (a cell refers to an area covered by one or more frequency resources). The BSS consists of:-

- BSC (Base Station Controller)
- BTS (Base Transmission Station)
- TC (Transcoder)

BSC (Base Station Controller)

The BSC is the central network element of BSS and it controls the radio network. It has several important tasks, some of which are presented in the following:

1. **Connection Establishment Between the MS and the NSS**:-All calls to and from the MS are connected through the group switch of the BSC (GSWB).
2. **Mobility Management**:-The BSC is responsibility for initiating the vast majority of all handovers, and it makes the handover decision based on, among others, measurement reports sent by the MS during a call.
3. **Statistical Raw Data Collection**
4. **Air-and-A-interface Signalling Support**:-In the A-interface, SS#7 (Common Channel Signalling System No. 7) is used as the signalling language, while the environment in the air interface allows the usage of a protocol adapted from language, while the environment in the air interface allows the usage of a protocol adapted from ISDN standards, namely LAP-Dm (Link Access Protocol on the ISDN D channel, modified version).

BTS (Base Transceiver Station)

The BTS is the network element responsibility for maintaining the air interface and minimizing the transmission problems (the air interface is very sensitive for disturbance). This task is accomplished with the help of some 120 parameters. The BTS has several very important tasks, some of which are presented in the following:

1. **Air Interface Signalling:** A lot of both call and non-call related signalling must be performed in order for the system of work. One examples is that when the MS is switched on for the every first time, it needs to send and receive and make Phone calls.
2. **Ciphering:** Both the BTS and the MS must be able to cipher and decipher information in order to protect the transmitted speech and data in the air interface.
3. **Speech Processing:** It refers to all the function the BTS performs in order to guarantee an error-free connection between the MS and the BTS. This includes task like speech coding, channel coding, and burst formatting.

TC (SM)-Transcoder (Sub Multiplexer)

In the air interface (between MS and BTS), the media carrying the traffic is a radio frequency. To enable an efficient transmission of digital speech information over the air interface, the digital speech signal is compressed. We must however also be able to communicate with and through the fixed network, where the speech compression format is different. Somewhere between the BTS and the fixed network, we therefore have to convert from one speech compression format to another, and this is where the Transcoder comes in.

NSS (Network Switching Subsystem)

It contains the network element MSC, VLR, HLR, AC and EIR. The main functions of NSS are:

- **Call Control:-**This identifies the subscriber, establishes a call, and clear the connection after the conversation is over.
- **Charging:-**This collects the charging information about a call and transfer it to billing centre.
- **Mobility Management:-**This maintains information about the subscriber's location.
- **Signalling:-**This applies to interface with the BSS and PSTN.
- **Subscriber Data Handling:-**This is the permanent data storage in the HLR and temporary storage of relevant data in the VLR.

MSC (Mobile Switching Centre)

The MSC is responsible for controlling calls in the mobile network. It identifies the origin and destination of a call, as well as the type of a call. An MSC acting as a bridge between a mobile network and fixed network is called a Gateway MSC. The MSC is responsible for:

- Call Control
- Initiation of Paging

VLR (Visitor Location Register)

It is a database which contains information about it subscriber's currently being in the service area of the MSC/VLR, such as:

- Identification numbers of the subscribers.
- Security information for authentication of the SIM card and for ciphering.
- Services that the subscriber can use.

HLR (Home Location Register)

It maintains a permanent register of the subscribers, for instance subscriber's identity numbers and the subscribed services. In addition to the fixed data, the HLR also keeps track of the current location of its customers. As you will see later, the MSC asks for routing information form the HLR. If a call I to be set up to a mobile station. In the Nokia implementation, the two network elements, AUC (Authentication Centre) and EIR (Equipment Identity Register) are located in the HLR.

AUC (Authentication Centre)

As for AC, the Equipment Identity Register is used for security reasons. But while the AC provides information for verifying the SIM cards, the EIR is responsible for IMEI checking.

EIR (Equipment Identity Register)

When performed, the mobile station is requested to provide the IMEI (International Mobile Equipment Identity) number. This number consists of type approval code, final assembly code and serial number of the mobile station.

The EIR contains three lists:-

- Mobile equipment in the white list is allowed to operate normally.
- If we suspect that a mobile equipment is finally, we can monitor the use of it.
- It is placed in the grey list.

- If the mobile equipment is reported stolen, or it is otherwise not allowed to operate in the network, it is placed in the black list.

CHAPTER SEVEN

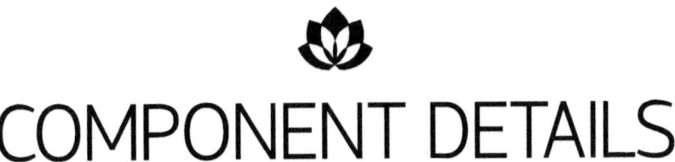

COMPONENT DETAILS

The components we will be using here can be brought from any of the online electronics stores which can be found on the internet. For this project we are going to use these following components.

COMPONENTS	QUANTITY
At mega 16	1
MT8870 I.C.	1
L293D I.C.	1
IN4007 Rectifier diode	1
100kilo-ohm Resistor	2
330kilo-ohm Resistor	1
10kilo-ohm Resistor	4
0.47 uF	1
22pF	4
0.1uF	1
Crystal (3.57MHz)	1
Crystal(12MHz)	1
Geared Motors	4
Battery(12V)	1

CHAPTER EIGHT

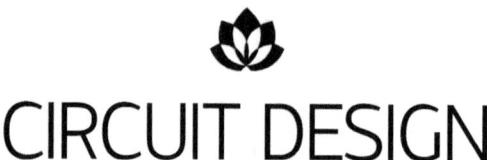

CIRCUIT DESIGN

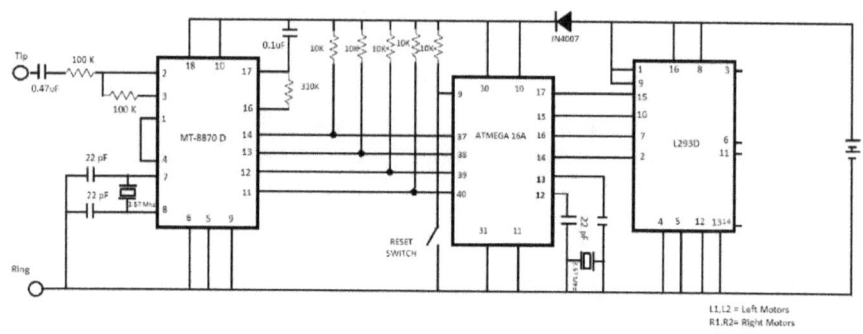

Circuit Design

CHAPTER NINE

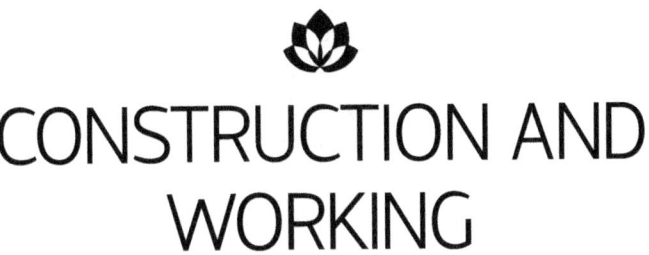

CONSTRUCTION AND WORKING

While constructing any unmanned vehicle one major mechanical constraint is the number of motors being used. We can have either a two wheel drive or a four-wheel drive. In general we have seen that though four-wheel drive is more complex than two-wheel drive, but it also provides more torque and good control. The circuit configuration shown in the previous section was built on a simple breadboard.

Motors are fixed to the bottom of this steel chassis and the circuit is affixed firmly on top of this chassis. A cell phone is also mounted on the chassis. In the four-wheel drive system, the two motors on a side are controlled independently of each other. So a single L293D driver IC can drive the unmanned car. In order to control the vehicle, we need to make a call to the cell phone attached to the vehicle from any phone, which sends DTMF tones on pressing the numeric buttons. The cell phone in the robotic car is kept in 'auto answer' mode. So after a ring, the cell phone accepts the call. Now we may press any button on our mobile to perform actions. The DTMF tones thus produced are received by the cell phone in the robot. These tones are fed to the circuit by the headset of the cell phone. Referring to our circuit diagram given we must note that the ring and tip in the circuit refers to the two wires that we get when we split open the headphone wire of any GSM phone. If we cut open the ear phone we will find 3 basic wires coming out: 1. Red wire (headset right output-Ring), 2. Blue wire (headset left output-Tip) and 3.Copper wire (ground wire). These are generally known as TRS headphone wires. Special care should be taken in this regard as these wires are laminated and the lamination must be removed before the wires are connected to the MT8870 DTMF decoder. Otherwise the tones will not be received effectively by the decoder.

The MT8870 decodes the received tone and sends the equivalent binary number to the microcontroller. According to the program in the microcontroller, the robot starts moving. Port D (PD0-PD7)) of Atmega16 has been designed as the output port of the microcontroller. We see that when key '2' is pressed on the mobile phone, the microcontroller outputs for forward motion. When we press key '8' on our mobile phone, the microcontroller outputs for reverse motion. When we press key '4' on our mobile phone, the microcontroller outputs for left direction motion. When we press key '6' on our mobile phone, the microcontroller outputs for right direction motion. Similarly when we press key '5' on our mobile phone, the microcontroller halts the vehicle. Five keys on the keypad are used for motion control of the unmanned car.

CHAPTER TEN

SOFTWARE DESIGN FRAMEWORK

The software is written in 'C' language and compiled using AVR Studio 6.0 'C' compiler. The source program is converted into hex code by the compiler. We burned this hex code into ATmega16 AVR microcontroller. Now, we will first describe the algorithm of the code structure, follow it up a control flow diagram and implement the algorithm in actual C code.

ALGORITHM

In this section we are going to discuss the working algorithm which we have used in the construction of the unmanned vehicle:

1. Include the register name defined specifically for ATmega16 and also declare the variable.
2. Set port A as the input and port D as the output.
3. The program will run forever by using 'while' loop.
4. Under 'while' loop, read port A and test the received input using 'switch' statement.
5. If 2 is pressed on the keypad, both the left and right motors move forward.
6. If 8 is pressed on the keypad, both the left and right motors moves backward.
7. If 4 is pressed on the keypad, the left motor halts and the right motor moves forward.
8. If 6 is pressed on the keypad, the right motor halts and the left motor moves forward.
9. If 5 is pressed on the keypad both the motors stop and the car comes to a stop.

10. The corresponding data will output at port D after testing and conditioning of the received data.

This was how we maneuverer our unmanned vehicle using our handheld mobile phone.

CHAPTER ELEVEN

CONTROL FLOW DIAGRAM

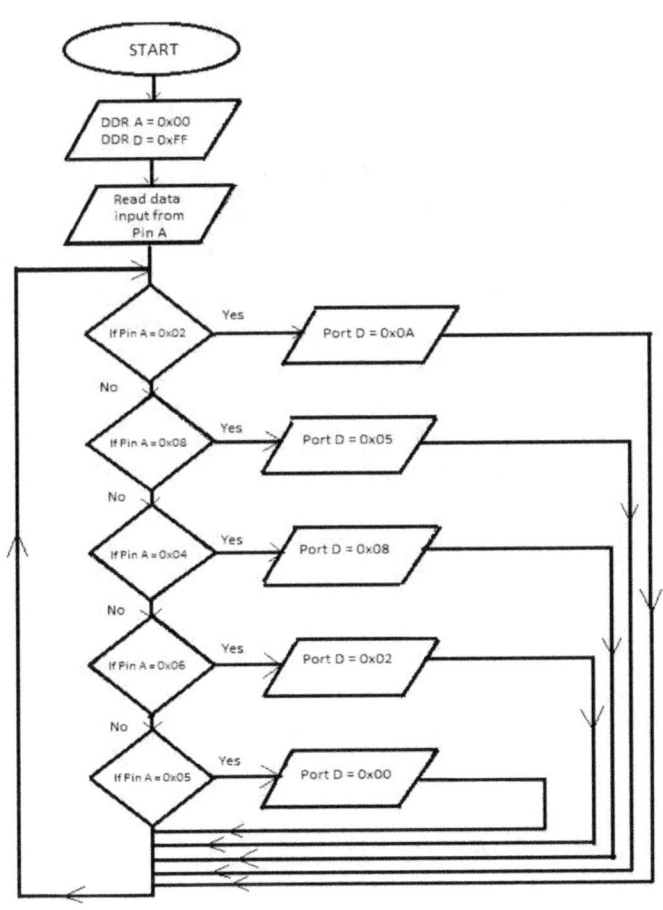

CHAPTER TWELVE

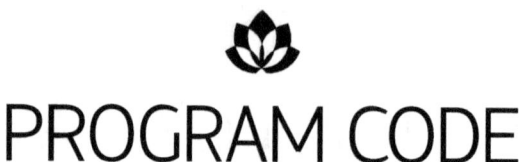

PROGRAM CODE

Here is the actual C code implementation:

```c
#include <avr/io.h> //standard I/O functions for ATMega16
int main(void)
{
unsigned int k;
DDRA= 0x00; // All pins of PORTA assigned as INPUT
DDRD=0xFF; // All pins of PORTD assigned as OUTPUT
PORTD=0x00; // All pins made to exhibit LOW state initially
while (1) // Infinite Loop
{
k=PINA; //Read Input from PINA
switch (k)
{
case 0x02: //BOT Moves forward
{
PORTD=0x0A; // Both Motors in Forward Direction
break;
}
case 0x08: // BOT Moves backward
{
PORTD=0x05; // Both Motors in Backward Direction
break;
}
case 0x04: //BOT Moves Left
{
PORTD=0x08; // RM-Forward and LM-Stop
break;
```

```
}
case 0x06: // BOT Moves Right
{
PORTD=0x02; // LM-Forward and RM-Stop
break;
}
case 0x05: // BOT Stops
{
PORTD=0x00; //Both left and right motors halt
break;
}
}
}
}
```

CHAPTER THIRTEEN

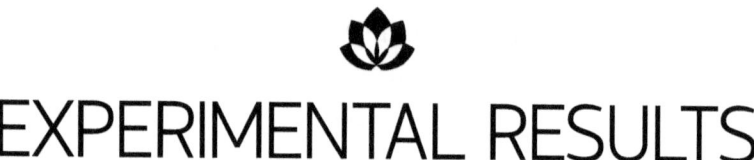

EXPERIMENTAL RESULTS

The HEX reading obtained from output pins of MT8870 and At mega 16.

KEY PRESSED	O/P OF MT-8870	I/P OF MICROCONTROLLER	O/P OF MICROCONTROLLER	DECISION TAKEN
2	0010	0010	0x0A	Forward
4	0100	0100	0x08	Left turn
6	0110	0110	0x02	Right turn
8	1000	1000	0x05	Backward
5	0101	0101	0x00	Stop

EXPERIMENTAL RESULTS

CHAPTER FOURTEEN

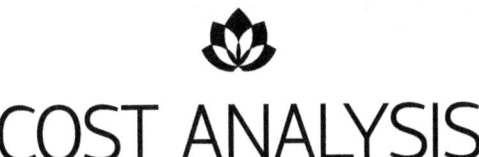

COST ANALYSIS

A comparative cost analysis is an integral part of any project that is carried out. In this section, we try to provide an approximate cost estimate of the project. The components used here can be brought from any of the online electronics stores which can be found on the internet. For this project we purchased the components i.e. AVR Atmega 16, L293D IC etc. from Amzon.com (Online Shopping Centre) and the rest could be found in local electronics market. We have listed the components and their prices in the following table:

COMPONENTS	QUANTITY	COST
At mega 16	1	₹ 899
MT8870 I.C.	1	₹ 499
L293D I.C.	1	₹ 500
IN4007 Rectifier diode	1	-
100kilo-ohm Resistor	2	-
330kilo-ohm Resistor	1	-
10kilo-ohm Resistor	4	-
0.47 uF	1	-
22pF	4	-
0.1uF	1	-
Crystal (3.57MHz)	1	₹ 10
Crystal(12MHz)	1	₹ 25
Geared Motors	4	₹ 1000
Battery(12V)	1	₹ 200

COST ESTIMATE

CHAPTER FIFTEEN

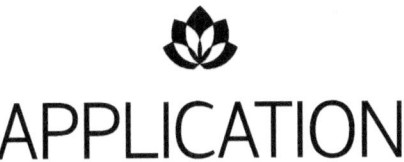

APPLICATION

APPLICATION

- **Scientific Use**

Recently, unmanned ground vehicles have found various scientific uses in hazardous and unknown environments. A lot of the probes which are sent to the other planets in our solar system have been unmanned ground vehicles, although some of the more recent ones were partially autonomous. The sophistication of these devices has fuelled greater debate on the need for manned spaceflight and exploration. For example, we see that the Voyager I spacecraft is the first craft of any kind to leave the solar system. The Martian explorers Spirit and Opportunity have provided us with continuous data about the surface of Mars since January 3, 2004. The efficiency and effectivity of these vehicles are also quite appreciable.

- **Military and Law Enforcement Use**

Military usage of remotely controlled military vehicles dates back to the first half of 20th century, when the Soviet Red Army used remotely controlled Tele tanks during 1930s in the Winter War and early stage of World War II. There were also remotely controlled cutters and experimental remotely controlled planes in the Red Army. Exposure to hazards is mitigated to the person who operates the vehicle from a location of relative safety. Remote controlled vehicles are used by many police department bomb-squads to defuse or detonate explosives. Unmanned Ground Vehicles (UGVs) have undergone a dramatic evolution in capability in the recent past. Early UGV's were capable of reconnaissance missions alone and but only with a limited range. Current UGV's can hover around possible targets until they are positively identified before releasing their payload of weaponry. Use of UGVs described in this paper can considerably improve upon the current structure.

- **Search and Rescue**

UGVs will also likely play an increased role in search and rescue missions. Slowly and steadily, all the developed nations (even some developing countries) are thinking about switching over and making use of these vehicles in case of natural disasters & emergencies. This can also be a great asset to save lives of both people along with soldiers in case of terrorist attacks like the one happened in 26 Nov, 2008 in Mumbai, India. The loss of military personnel can be largely reduced by using these advanced vehicles. This was demonstrated by the successful use of USVs during the 2008 hurricanes that struck Louisiana and Texas.

- **Agriculture**

UGVs are one type of agricultural robot. Unmanned harvesting tractors can be operated around the clock making it possible to handle short windows for harvesting. UGVs are also used for spraying and thinning. They can also be used to monitor the health of crops and livestock.

- **Civilian and Commercial applications**

Multiple civilian applications of UGVs are being implemented to automatic processes in manufacturing and production environments. They have also been developed as autonomous tour guides for the Carnegie Museum of Natural History and the Swiss National Exhibition Expo.

- **Manufacturing**

In the manufacturing environment, UGVs are used for transporting materials. They are often automated and referred to as AGVs. Aerospace companies use these vehicles for precision positioning and transporting heavy, bulky pieces between manufacturing stations, which are less time-consuming than using large cranes and can keep people from engaging with dangerous areas.

- **Mining**

UGVs can be used to traverse and map mine tunnels. Combining radar, laser, and visual sensors, UGVs are in development to map 3D rock surfaces in open pit mines.

- **Supply Chain**

In the warehouse management system, UGVs have multiple uses from transferring goods with autonomous forklifts and conveyors to stock scanning and taking inventory.

- **Space Application**

NASA's Mars Exploration Rover project includes two UGVs, Spirit and Opportunity, that are still performing beyond the original design parameters. This is attributed to redundant systems, careful handling, and long-term interface decision making. Opportunity (rover) and its twin, Spirit (rover), six-wheeled, solar powered ground vehicles, were launched in July 2003 and landed on opposite sides of Mars in January 2004. The Spirit rover operated nominally until it became trapped in deep sand in April 2009, lasting more than 20 times longer than expected. Opportunity, by comparison, has been operational for more than 12 years beyond its intended lifespan of three months. Curiosity (rover) landed on Mars in September 2011, and its original two-year mission has since been extended indefinitely.

- **Forest Conservation**

In the recent times, the wildlife has been prone to serious endangerment. Many animals are on the verge of becoming extinct, including the tiger to name a few. The spy robotic car can really be of help to us in this purpose. Since it is a live streaming device and also mobile, it can keep the forest guards constantly updated and alerted about the status of the different areas of the forest which are prone to attack.

CHAPTER SIXTEEN

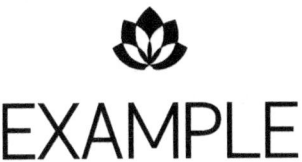

EXAMPLE

Examples
  SARGE
  SARGE is based on a 4-wheel drive all-terrain vehicle, the frame of the Yamaha Breeze. Currently, the objective is to provide each infantry battalion with up to eight SARGE units (Singer, 2009b). The SARGE robot is primarily used for remote surveillance; sent ahead of the infantry to investigate potential ambushes.
  Multi-Utility Tactical Transport
  Built by General Dynamics Land Systems, the Multi-Utility Tactical Transport (MUTT) comes in 4-, 6- and 8-wheeled variants. It is currently being trialled by the US military.
  X-2
  X-2 is medium sized tracked UGV built by Digital Concepts Engineering. It is based on a previous autonomous robotic system designed for use in EOD, search and rescue (SAR), perimeter patrol, communications relay, mine detection and clearing, and as light weapons platform. It measures 1.31 m in length, weighs 300kg and can reach speeds of 5 km/h. It will also traverse slopes up to 45' steep and cross deep mud. The vehicle is controlled using the Marionette system which is also used on Wheelbarrow EOD robots.
  The Warrior
  A new model of the PackBot was also produced, known as the Warrior. It is over five times the size of a PackBot, can travel at speeds of up to 15 mph, and is the first variation of a PackBot capable of carrying a weapon (Singer, 2009a). Like the PackBot, they play a key role in checking for explosives. They are capable of carrying 68 kilograms, and travelling at 8 MPH. The Warrior is priced at nearly 400,000 and more than 5000 units have already been delivered worldwide.

TerraMax

The TerraMax UVG package is designed to be integrated into any tactical wheeled vehicle, and is fully incorporated into the brakes, steering, engine and transmission. Fitted vehicles retain the ability to be driver-operated. Vehicles manufactured by Oshkosh Defence and fitted with the package have competed in the DARPA Grand Challenges of 2004 and 2005, and the DARPA Urban Challenge of 2007. The Marine Corps Warfighting Lab selected TerraMax-equipped MTVRs for the Cargo UGV project initiated in 2010, culminating in a technology concept demonstration for the Office of Naval Research in 2015. Demonstrated uses for the upgraded vehicles include unmanned route clearance (with a mine roller) and reducing personnel required for transportation convoys.

The Talon

The Talon is primarily used for bomb disposal, and was incorporated with the ability to be waterproof at 100ft so that it can search the seas for explosives as well. The Talon was first used in 2000, and over 3,000 units have been distributed worldwide. By 2004, The Talon had been used in over 20,000 separate missions. These missions largely consisted of situations were considered to be too dangerous for humans (Carafano & Gudgel, 2007). These can include entering booby-trapped caves, searching for IEDs, or simply scouting a red combat zone. The Talon is one of the fastest Unmanned Ground Vehicles on the market, easily keeping pace with a running soldier. It can operate for 7 days off of one charge, and is even capable of climbing stairs. This robot was used at Ground Zero during the recovery mission. Like its peers, the Talon was designed to be incredibly durable. According to reports, one unit fell off of a bridge into a river and the soldiers simply turned on the control unit and drove it out of the river.

Swords Robot

Shortly after the release of the Warrior, the SWORDS robot was designed and deployed. It is a Talon robot with an attached weapon system. SWORDS is capable of mounting any weapon weighing less than 300 pounds. In a matter of seconds, the user can fit weapons such as a grenade launcher, rocket launcher, or 0.50 inch (12.7 mm) machine gun. Moreover, the SWORDS can use their weapons with extreme precision, hitting the bull's-eye of a target 70/70 times. These robots are capable of withstanding a lot of damage, including multiple 0.50 inch bullets, or a fall from a helicopter onto concrete. In addition, the SWORDS robot is even capable of making its way through virtually any terrain, including underwater. In 2004, only four SWORDS units were in existence although 18 were requested for service overseas. It was named as one of the world's most amazing inventions by Time Magazine in 2004. The US Army deployed three to Iraq in 2007 but then cancelled support of the project.

Small Unit Mobility Enhancement Technology (SUMET)

The SUMET system is a platform and hardware independent, low-cost electro-optical perception, localization, and autonomy package developed to convert a traditional vehicle into a UGV. It performs various autonomous logistics manoeuvres in austere/harsh off-road environments, without dependence on a human operator or on GPS. The SUMET system has been deployed on several different tactical and commercial platforms and is open, modular, scalable and extensible.

Autonomous Small Scale Construction Machine (ASSCM)

The ASSCM is a civilian unmanned ground vehicle developed in Yuzuncu Yil University by scientific project granted by TUBITAK (Project code 110M396). The vehicle is a low cost small scale construction machine which can grade soft soil. The machine is capable of autonomously grading the earth within a polygon once the border of the polygon is defined. The machine determines its position by CP-DGPS and direction by consecutive position measurements. Currently the machine can autonomously grade simple polygons. The autonomous grading algorithm and control system of the machine are developed.

CHAPTER SEVENTEEN

EMERGENCY RESPONSE

UGVs are used in many emergency situations including urban search and rescue, firefighting, and nuclear response. Following the 2011 Fukushima Daiichi Nuclear Power Plant accident, UGVs were used in Japan for mapping and structural assessment in areas with too much radiation to warrant a human presence.

Military Applications

UGV use by the military has saved many lives. Applications include explosive ordnance disposal (EOD) such as landmines, loading heavy items, and repairing ground conditions under enemy fire. The number of robots used in Iraq increased from 150 in 2004 to 5000 in 2005 and they disarmed over 1000 roadside bombs in Iraq at the end of 2005 (Carafano & Gudgel, 2007). By 2013, the U.S. Army had purchased 7,000 such machines and 750 had been destroyed. The military is using UGV technology to develop robots outfitted with machine guns and grenade launchers that may replace soldiers.

CHAPTER EIGHTEEN

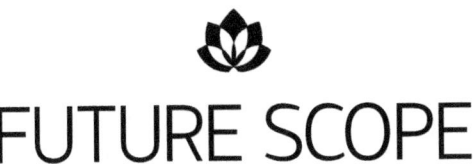

FUTURE SCOPE

The design procedure of an unmanned surface vehicle as presented in this paper can be further extended to include IR sensors and also a system to include password protection for the USV.IR sensors can be used to automatically detect & avoid obstacles if the vehicle goes beyond line of sight. Thisavoids damage to the vehicle if we are manoeuvring it from a distant place. Project can be modified in order to password protect the vehicle so that it can be operated only if correct password is entered. Either cell phone should be password protected or necessary modification should be made in the assembly language code. This introduces conditioned access and increases security to a great extent. In case the vehicle is used as a spy car, a camera can also be mounted on the car. Such basic improvements can be made on the existing system as and when the requirement arises without making any major changes in the principle design of the USV.

CHAPTER NINETEEN

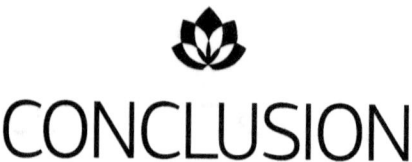

CONCLUSION

By developing such an unmanned surface vehicle, we have overcome the drawbacks of the conventionally used RF circuits. This RCV includes advantages such as robust control, minimal interference and a large working range. The car requires five commands for motion control. The remaining controls are available to serve purposes dependant on the area of application of the RCV. We have tried to reduce the circuit complexity and improve upon the human machine interface. The cost analysis of the project described in section VII of this paper clearly indicates a huge improvement in the cost expenditure of the production of these unmanned vehicles. Moreover handling these USVs does not require much skill on the part of the user. Even an ordinary person can manoeuvre these USVs without having to know much about the internal circuitry. In this way the cost involved in training people to use such USVs can also be saved.

CHAPTER TWENTY

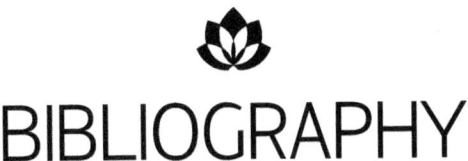

BIBLIOGRAPHY

- L. Schenker, "Pushbutton Calling with a Two- Group Voice-Frequency Code", The Bell System Technical Journal, 39(1), 1960, 235–255, ISSN 0005-8580
- Abah O. Sunday, Visa M. Ibrahim, Abah Joshua," Remote Control of Electrical Appliances Using GSM Networks", International Journal of Engineering Research and Development, Volume 1, Issue 9 (June 2012), PP.38-45, ISSN: 2278-067X
- S. A. Nasar, I. Boldea, Electric Drives (CRC/Taylor and Francis, 2006)
- V. Subramanyam, Electric Drives (Mc-Graw Hill, 1996)
- T. M. Ladwa, S. M. Ladwa, and R. S. Kaarthik, A. R. Dhara, and N.Dalei, "Control of Remote Domestic System Using DTMF," presented at ICICI-BME 2009 Bandung, Indonesia, 2009.
- Y. C. Cho and J. W. Jeon, "Remote Robot control System based on DTMF of Mobile Phone," IEEE International Conference INDIN, 2008, July 2008.
- M. Callahan Jr., "Integrated DTMF Receiver," IEEE Transactions on communications, vol. 27, pp. 343-348, February 1979.
- R. Sharma, K. Kumar, and S. Viq, "DTMF Based Remote Control System," IEEE International Conference ICIT 2006, pp. 2380-2383, December 2006.
- Edwin Wise, Robotics Demystified (Mc-Graw Hill, 2005)

www.ingramcontent.com/pod-product-compliance
Lightning Source LLC
Chambersburg PA
CBHW070838220526
45466CB00002B/816